The Right to Vote

By Tracy Vonder Brink

Table of Contents

THE RIGHT TO VOTE 3
WORDS TO KNOW.................................22
INDEX 23
COMPREHENSION QUESTIONS 23
ABOUT THE AUTHOR.................................24

A Starfish Book

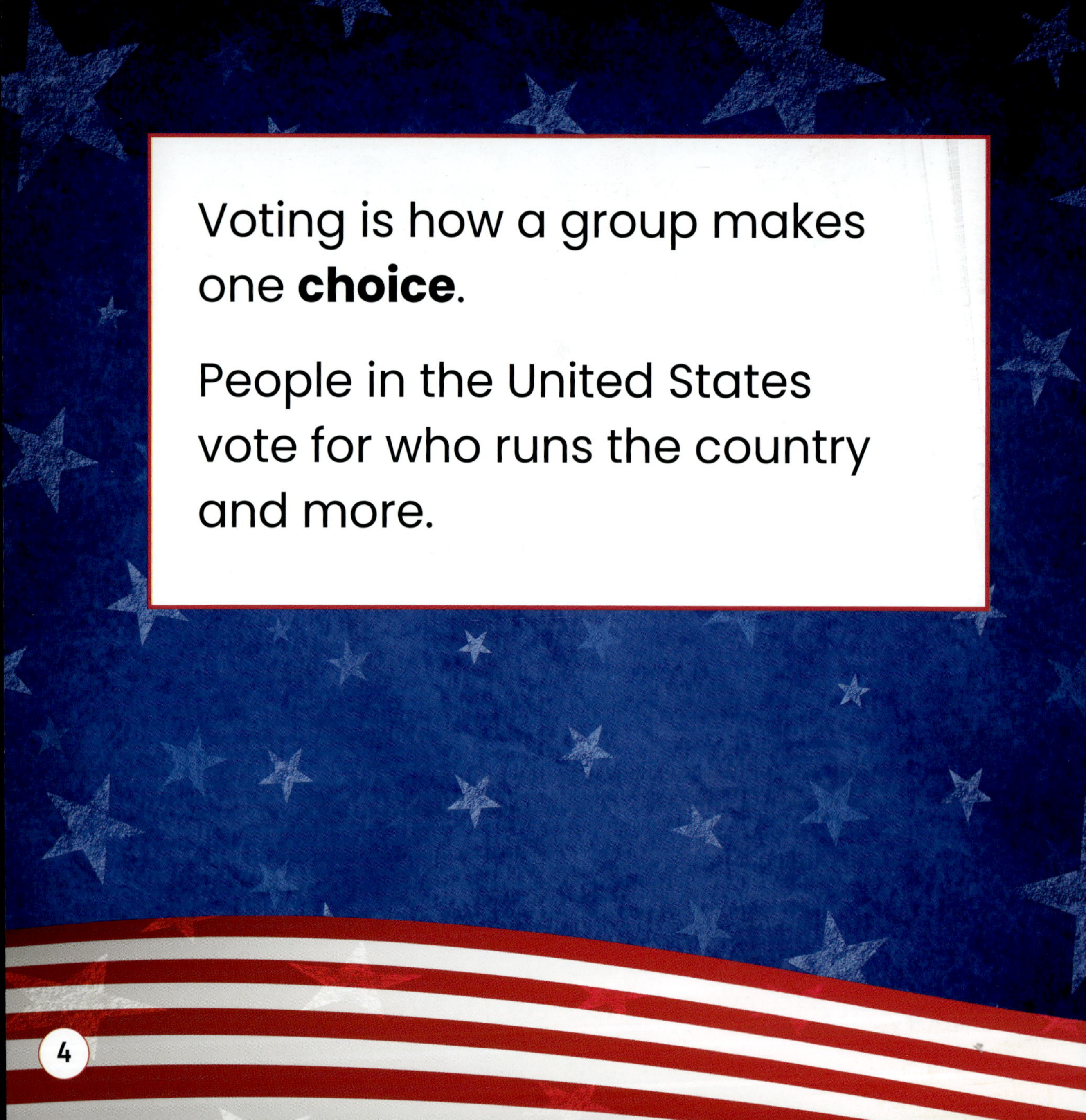

Voting is how a group makes one **choice**.

People in the United States vote for who runs the country and more.

Teaching Tips for Caregivers:

As a caregiver, you can help your child succeed in school by giving them a strong foundation in language and literacy skills and a desire to learn to read.

This book helps children grow by letting them practice reading skills.

Reading for pleasure and interest will help your child to develop reading skills and will give your child the opportunity to practice these skills in meaningful ways.

- Encourage your child to read on her own at home
- Encourage your child to practice reading aloud
- Encourage activities that require reading
- Establish a reading time
- Talk with your child
- Give your child writing materials

Teaching Tips for Teachers:

Research shows that one of the best ways for students to learn a new topic is to read about it.

Before Reading

- Read the "Words to Know" and discuss the meaning of each word.
- Read the back cover to see what the book is about.

During Reading

- When a student gets to a word that is unknown, ask them to look at the rest of the sentence to find clues to help with the meaning of the unknown word.
- Ask the student to write down any pages of the book that was confusing to them.

After Reading

- Discuss the main idea of the book.
- Ask students to give one detail that they learned in the book by showing a text dependent answer from the book.

The Right to Vote

The teacher says, "Let's **vote** on today's snack!"

The class chooses to have grapes.

Bugs in My Yard

Kim Thompson

TABLE OF CONTENTS

Sight Words.......... 2
Words to Know.......... 3
Index.......... 16

A Pelican Book

Teaching Tips for Caregivers and Teachers:

Research shows that one of the best ways for students to learn a new topic is to read about it.

Before Reading

- Read the title and predict what the book will be about.
- Read the "Words to Know" and discuss the meaning of each word.
- Read the back cover to see what the book is about.

During Reading

- When a student gets to a word that is unknown, ask them to look at the rest of the sentence to find clues to help with the meaning of the unknown word.
- Motivate students with praise and encouragement.

After Reading

- Discuss the main idea of the book.
- Ask students to give one detail that they learned in the book.

Sight Words

a	fly	little
away	go	make
can	have	what
find	in	you

flower

You can find a little **bee**!

bee

Bees have **wings**.

wing

Bees go in a **beehive**.

beehive

Bees make **honey**.

honey

A bee can fly away!

Index

bee(s) 6, 7, 8, 10, 12, 14
find 4, 6
fly 14
honey 12, 13
little 6
make 12

Written by: Kim Thompson
Design by: Under the Oaks Media
Series Development: James Earley

Photos: herain Kanthatham: cover; Anton Nikitinskiy: p. 5; Jack Hong: p. 7; Mircea Costina: p. 9; nicemyphoto: p. 11; STARsoft: p. 13; ETgohome: p. 15

Library of Congress PCN Data
Bees / Kim Thompson
Bugs in My Yard
ISBN 978-1-63897-424-6(hard cover)
ISBN 978-1-63897-539-7(paperback)
ISBN 978-1-63897-654-7(EPUB)
ISBN 978-1-63897-769-8(eBook)
Library of Congress Control Number: 2021953297
Printed in the United States of America.

Seahorse Publishing Company
www.seahorsepub.com 1-800-387-7650

Published in the United States
Seahorse Publishing
PO Box 771325
Coral Springs, FL 33077